Over Here

Alan Gillis

OVER HERE

Wake Forest University Press

First North American edition

First published in Ireland by The Gallery Press in July 2025. Edited by Peter Fallon.

For permission, write to
Wake Forest University Press
Post Office Box 7333
Winston-Salem, NC 27109
wfupress.wfu.edu
wfupress@wfu.edu

ISBN 978-1-943667-23-9 (paperback)
Library of Congress Control Number 2026940169

Cover design and typesetting by Shannon Pallatta

Printed in Canada

Publication of this book was generously supported by the Boyle Family Fund.

in memory of Michael Longley

Contents

Whin

Ruined greens, thistle-pokes, here I am
lost again under grey Y-front skies
where tired mustard splotches of gorse,
nicotine-stained shocks of furze,

bristle in a ring like Aunties circling
at a wake with tea-leaf teeth muttering,
'All that is eternal fears fulfilment.'
Then the sky splits open in a flash-flood

of sun glare and the whin bursts
marigold-gleam, lemon-dazzled honey
as white-green winged butterflies
ripple over purple swaying heather.

Aye, this is me. Here. Among fuzz
blossom, thorn blooms, wild coconut
whiffs, a far-gone goat bleating,
'Dew on the grass, light in your eye!'

The Desk

Often I'm sat at this desk.
It's OK. Deskwork lets me put
bread on the table, and it's not
as if I'm chained to the desk
in my mind. Oh no, I can be anywhere.

I'm usually walking down a local
kind of street with shops,
a bit of leafage, uncrowded
yet populated with everyone
not noticing me in a cool, normal way.

I could be in the Museo de Altamira in Santillana del Mar
or on a tiny vessel upon the West Atlantic's
greenblack swells with madcap bluefin tuna.
But that can prove distracting.
So I'm mostly walking

this local street in my mind
when I'm at my desk.
Frequently I must click on a message
and sometimes when I do
the ground beneath my desk gives way.

It's not that the heart leaps,
more that the abdomen shoots forty feet
into the air while the torso plummets.
Or I click on a message
and they are coming for me

with implements.
Through the night over plains
across the city in a beat-up white van
they are coming
and I wish I'd never clicked on that message.

But, mostly, people are sat in a pleasant
pavement-side café seating area
doing their thing
and I'm going somewhere natural.
When yet another message pings

I wonder if it's the desk itself
messaging to remind me I'm sat at a desk,
like God putting Jonah in his place.
Or perhaps it's Trevor from Head Office
reasserting the hierarchy.

If you rest your head upon a desk
with eyes up to the surface
for long enough it becomes vast,
interdimensional
like outer space or how a coffin

lid might be, if you're in the coffin
for long enough.
But I am on my street
and I am going to the meadows.
The air hums with unread

messages, the short light wings
of blue tits, furze spines,
my insides like willowherb
lifted in the breeze.
I am going often at my desk.

Midsummer

Here we are still, after all this time.
Windows in the tall flats that face our house
gleam like a buttercup under the chin.
Our garden has the same few trees that bend
but don't shift, though I like to imagine
they rise in the night, stretch with a groan
and mosey about, shoot the breeze,
before returning to their roots at dawn.

We've hung a bird feeder from a branch
where hedge sparrows go crazy for the seed.
Furious, really, but they lift the heart.
Elderly neighbours, for many of whom
passing through the threshold is an episode,
shuffle to the corner shop past rowans,
litter and snapdragon, muttering
to themselves in imagined conversations

like this one. A bluebottle foothers
at the window, as if small things are free,
while sunlight on wheelie bins and grass
falls in such a way it makes you wonder.
A hedge sparrow says, 'I won't lie to you.'
At night I hear multistreams, stoners, foxes
under phone masts, moths on dark lilies.
'Here's the way it is,' say the trees.

The Tomato

The big juicy tomato
grows red but not quite red
as tomato ketchup. Off the vine
is it dead or just beginning
to die? It's a big ripe juicy tomato

anyhow—succulacious and uneven
scarlet with olive hints, tinged yellows:
its watery pulp, seeded liquid, swollen
in filmy skin. The way it catches light
it looks like light gleams from within.

Tomatoes were tastier at yours—
where I tagged along through allotment
rows to the sun-gilt of your green-
house windows—each year from nothing
to squelchous bites of tomatoey wow.

Now you're gone. I see a million jars
of tomato sauce on shelves, vats of ooze,
dismal dinner bowls, mouth-slurp stains.
Here is plenty, with rot in it.
A shovel leans against the unlatched door,

drones of greenfly in the late sun—
I'm back among the greenhouse rows
where you once sang to your growbags:
Lass, shall I go with you to the meadow?
And here it comes again—that tingle

on the tongue for a taste of another
salt-tanged, sour-vibrant, juice-burst
red sunrise. It is fantastic with mayo.
Dusk falls on the allotments.
Sing for your life. Sing for a tomato.

The Umbrellas

One wet day I was young, head in pieces,
I found myself in a Dublin gallery
weighed down yet windblown-minded,
where I came upon Renoir's *Umbrellas.*
Its blue shades and swimming greys—
somewhere between a hug and hallucination—
swerved and swooned to reveal
faces are infinite and everything curves

which brought to mind one wet night,
younger still, on the slopes of Scrabo's
furze and warren holes and long views
with my head in bits, the whole shebang
a horror, when I heard whispering trees,
airs from nowhere as if the night
was weaving me—the night-lights of Ards
a blur of brushstrokes over Strangford Lough.

Now I'm past it, my head's a bomb scare,
all I know is the truth cannot be known
but encountered, and art is an umbrella.
As rain falls, I take my stand here
this soaked August, under the sycamore:
this city of seed pods, twisted old-rooter,
this birdsong jukebox with two hundred
thousand green tongues French kissing the air.

The Commute

I'm trying to get back to Dublin,
the one I lived in years ago—
the view from Patrick Street
looking over Dublin on a snow-
bound December—though I know
that Dublin is unreal now.

I'm drifting off somewhere
near the border on a train
where a man waits in the aisle
for the vacant seat next to me
but I'm miles away. Some place
down a rowan-lined lane.

And the man is vexed waiting,
tapping my shoulder to shift
over for him. He is dead
peeved and I see the rowan-lined
lane fill with snow as the train
speeds through same-again suburbs.

The man fingers his device
and the next stop is not mine
but I find myself walking through
avenues lined with rowans.
Then I come to. Snow
drifts and blurs the window

as if in the middle of a memory
wipe on a train where the man
taps, taps and everyone
blends into a scroll of light
speeding into Dublin but not
getting there because there's no stop

The Queensferry Bridge

Dwarfed by the construction, I drive towards
this big new bridge: its cathedral of gleam
a vast suspended gesture through the air.
Even this approach road is so large-scale
I feel I'm driving a miniature toy,

half-expecting a gigantic child's hand
will loom down to grab and raise my Honda
to its beatific laughing mega-face
in the sky. And each coming glimpse
of the bridge brings a lift in expectation

of the Firth's expansion and Fife's green
coast, for these days in the city have left me
feeling like one of those gratuitous
extended scenes on the box where some guy
punches and punches and punches

a face to death. Now I'm finally crossing
the bridge, I am high if not free above
water that looks how I imagine the mind
might look if it were visible: a sky-
coloured brim-swill of wave glint and shadow,

all ambivalent surface and unseen
depth currents, immense inner convections
that could arise, if aroused, swallow
the coast and crush this bridge. I can't wait
to drive by Fife's warehouses and housing

schemes with tricycles on the lawn,
oven chips in the oven, bay windows
looking out to sea waves, purple milkvetch,
creeping buttercup, common selfheal and oil
rigs that straddle dream-blue waters.

Yet I'm still crossing the bridge as the wind
pummels and pummels and pummels.
Traffic is fast, but this feels like a queue.
I'm crossing the bridge towards fish
and chips in East Neuk, blind curves in the road,

eroding shores that leave me feeling
like the misted salt-spawn of waves
as they smash and smash and smash
upon rocks, sprayed into raw air,
traffic fuming through this glittering metal

thrust into the Firth that I'm almost across,
hoping something might come, some new thought,
better feeling. For the mind is the sea,
the mind is mountains, rivers, and the great earth
moving and suspended until it's not.

Suspended

1

My thoughts are like thought-
balloons, or beachballs
with peach, orange, green, purple polka dots
bouncing, bouncing in an empty shopping mall.

2

Warhol's *Silver Clouds* were a charm
for a while; until the penny dropped
I would never, shall never leave that room.
And still I bounce, waft, hover, and, like, flop.

3

My daughter smiles, her head in a screen.
My wife frowns, her head in a screen.
My son ... whatever, his head in a screen.
And *I'm* the one adrift, floating, awake or in a dream.

4

Finally, the poem was complete. 'It's about time,'
she said. Well, at least it's about something.

Self-Reflection in a Window of the Free Presbyterian Church

I took a shortcut down a dark path to Domino's
because getting parked near there's a no-no
and my kids had been promised pizza as a treat
and were barking for it back home, so the threat
of their carping was in my head as I weighed
up the safe, but long, way around beneath red
streetlights, against that narrow shortcut lane
by a black stone church. So it was hard to explain,
later, why I came home with no Ranch BBQ
pizza, no Ben & Jerry's Caramel Chew Chew,
face white as a Rizzla, reaching straight for the malt.
I dropped it all under a hedgerow's pelt
of thorns. 'He came at me,' I said, to my wife's tuts,
'through the church window ... looked out of his nut.'

The Song Thrush

I

Aware of the need to calm
the kids' mounting climate anxiety
but unsure how to balance their need for fact against the reality
those facts will scare the screaming blue Jesus out of them

I tried putting it into song:
we've fecked it all—*keep on going,*
irreversible, accelerating—*keep on going,*
unevenly distributed catastrophic effects—*just keep on …*
   aye, it came out wrong.

My youngest smiles and gets on, but in her den
I see her—fixing on somewhere about an inch
beyond the map of the world on her wall of pink gloss paint

with all the twitchy premonition and weird zen
of a song thrush on a juniper branch
in woodland marked for housing development.

2

To find our way, we leave our estate and enter
a stream of Diesels, EVs, Hybrids, V8s, driving around
a six-road roundabout, then park by the household
waste recycling centre's skips of polyester,

laminates, rusting refrigerators, fragments of home.
We walk past Greggs bags, Costa cups
blown by the wind, needles, takeaway slops
over council grass, dandelions and celandine,

a playpark of shattered bottles, then pass
through a gate into woodland where we find
ourselves between leaf-swish and chiffchaff

on colour-coded walkways among nettle-moods,
hazel-shades, bug-twitches and buck mad
electric scooters on a cycle path where thrushes laugh.

3

We walk into the wood's hushed
river-sound of birch leaves, willow warblers,
flathead yellowhammers and a song thrush
in full song through white-pink hawthorn flowers.

A killjoy might ask, little bird, how
do you do it? Without
a care for carbon gigatonne targets
you just eat and bobble and sing and fly.

Still we cling to our dream of those far gone
affirmations, the wood's looping church
choir, dragonflies among bluebells, fat green

caterpillars contemplating the change,
dank mushroom banks, fungal skies and great oaks
where thrushes launch, borne into the flux.

4

It's easy to feel the whole woodland is one
big nest when circled by trees, the *cheep-chirps*
of a song thrush. Or skylark? I need a birdsong app.
Birches root us in the hug of deeper home.

I say, 'I could wrap myself in leaves and lay
in a hidey-hole of bracken, moss, snug in a hollow.'
'Aye, you could,' says our kid, 'so long as there's an espresso
machine and wifi.' We go our separate ways

for a while. 'And heating, and plumbing, and sausage rolls …'
her singsong voice. 'The problem with your gen …'
I begin, but her path slopes off and I flump

past elm and spruce, thrushes tweeting 'arsehole'
in happy songs at the end of the world again.
When our paths reconverge she says, 'Och, cheer up!'

5

It's hard to be anything
other than a doomster, but we're lifted by the swooshed pines
of this woodland, in and out of our minds,
its comedy of squirrels, moss-bed squelch, ladybird throng.

'Let us appreciate what's here and work from there,'
we agree. 'What use are we overwhelmed?'
So we partake of green glints, the clearing's wham
of primrose, sorrel, swoons of juniper,

wren song woven with tweets from a song thrush,
brook trickle, snowdrops, common blues, birch leaves
in the wood's tangled rolling music and hush.

It's hard to get your head around extinction.
It's hard to believe
the sun does not love what it lights upon.

Haar

See how you feel? Once I saw
nothing but weak-piss light on a tattoo
of blue grey and grey blue
bleak stone, black stone, bletched sandstone.

I saw buildings of flu-grey granite
loom over paving flags of bilge
beneath a sky of cold porridge.
The city looked encrypted:

tall buildings were rows of crypts
raised high on blunt force—
pitch your head against the surface
of Edinburgh and your skull will split.

I saw a demented gull's slice of meat
feast pizza fall from the air onto a cardboard
mattress and stained clump of sleeping bag
outside a letting agency on Clerk Street.

I saw an up-comer posting updates
from his run through Holyrood Park
with smart-filtered panoramic shots
of the city captioned *#thisplaceisgreat!!!*

I saw a local in puff
jacket with papier-mâché skin
knocking her head off a Pharmacy door muttering
fck this, fck fck, fck you, fck off ...

Then things turned grim: streets gloomed,
the way the mind can cloud and memories
vanish, as the air
thickened to virtual mushroom.

A thick haar began to doom-
scroll over the pelt of Arthur's Seat
to swallow Parliament,
Dynamic Earth, South Side, Moredun

in flumes of virus-grey shadow.
Some retro Gothic film maker
would have paid a million to catch its spectral
fingers groping through the Meadows.

I saw a child pointing 'Look at this!'
as the fog rubbed against her flat window
while an elderly couple, at the window below,
were deleted by the uncoiling mist.

I could hear unseen buses drive
as if ferryboats chugging in a cosmic ladle
of unspeakable soup—faint lanterns
through a fog that seemed unalive.

It felt like hard things were feather-
blown through a nimbostratus
of dream: banks, firms, start-ups, statues
blipped in a continuous aether.

I saw each building was a vessel
adrift in an ocean of haze—
Edinburgh a ghost fleet of container
ships, carriers of counted souls.

I could see nothing is out there
to separate us from the infinite
void of space—not bricks,
steel, concrete—but atmosphere.

I could see that each room, each lair
is a nest of fragile bones, breaths,
skin types, needs, body reeks, regrets,
cells at the mercy of the air.

I could see how truly we share
our element with the dead
in limbo, how this total cloud
blinds all here

in a womb of haze-rain,
the walls like pulsing membranes,
where I try to find my way home
through the reek and fire in these stones.

December in Edinburgh

Young people have hung
themselves from oaks.
Some are running to the dark
away from harm.

Winds gulder through Moredun,
trees flayed to the bone.
Come home, come home.
In Hawkhill Woods

frozen paths, crunched underfoot,
give onto sludge.
Hawthorn crackles and shivers.

The moon over Craigmillar
casts a kerosene light
over juniper and ash and spurge.

Young Team

I

Like all children
he was a lozenge
of sun.

When he smiled
those he lit upon
were red campion

or ox-eye daisies
in a grass meadow.
But boys grow

radge and squinny-
eyed in schemes
at the edge of the edge of the edge of understanding.

2

He smashed the furniture
in his mind.
Then the furniture.

Big hole in the door,
knuckles frayed.

You can see through to a dark corridor.
Or look the other way,
a young lad slumped on the floor.

3

tracksuit in the rain
        teacher says is 'unsuited for the rain'
    ice winds that cut stripes through
            skin and bones and fuck you

walls look like walls
        great big manky monkey balls
    walls look like walls
            words fuzzed on the blackboard

'what are you here for?'
        teacher says wherefore therefore
    well—I'm well-out fucko
            so shove yer mumbo le jumbo

spinning me round round round till I throw
        up and now I'm frozen—ach! let it go
    the pills are kicking in and the lamp-
            posts look like security in shops

walkie-talkies on the warpath
        teacher asking 'have you seen a bath?'
    walls scowling like textbooks at this fruit-loop
            walky-talky ice pop in a tracksuit

no wanting to be a twat
        left hanging   LOOK! the full moon!
    up in the sky   HEY THERE! big moon
            what yah looking at?

4

The names for things buzz.
Words flicker and blur and dance
off each page. It's hard to make sense
of how one thing follows another
when everything cross-wiggles and inter-things.

Once I saw a pillow's-worth of feathers
scatter and drift and whirl and fall
from nowhere to the pavement.
One step. Two step. One step. At a time.

Each time I go forwards—a wee flutter
in case my foot doesn't meet concrete
but takes a plunge through nothing
solid. The wind upsets the leaves
in the trees. No one notices. Then they leave.

When You Are Old

When you are old, knackered and stressed
steal a night for yourself, fill your glass,
your screen with yesterday's photos and texts,
download this poem, slowly read these lines
and dream of yourself, your green summer dress.

Dream of how free you felt, light on your feet.
Dream of how they followed you like bees
craving the crocus, your likes their sunshine;
how one lost soul wrote you curious verse
and you messaged *LOL ♥ some other time!*

Then dream of how, when tomorrow came,
Time slipped from your bedside, stole your purse,
your devices, tiptoed out the door and ran
laughing down the cold morning street.

Notations from the Care Home Common Room

He prefers a Toyota. It's a terrible muddle.
Family's in Bakhmut city. Found a spot on the lung.
Not a jot, not one iota. Last time was murder.
A worldwide worry. The sun sets like a song.

No sense, but what melody. Two rabbits, a goat, a
ferret as skinny as it's long. Imagine the indignity.
A blackbird in the tree? Well, it's not on the rota.
Nurse worse than King Kong. The sun sets like whiskey.

Not Swedish, Finnish. And a fourteen-inch pizza.
That Prius is some machine. The shih-tzu's doolally.
Eh ... uhm ... mmm ... eeesh. Either the council or mafia.
Looking for the mean. The sun sets like a memory

at the onset of night's dementia. Sponge, cherries, cream.
Her mind's a midden. Left lying like a jellyfish.
There's an app for trauma. A ninny, a moonbeam.
Try to find the middle. The sun sets, and we're finished.

The Gulf of St Vincent

in memory of Margaret Townsend

'Ten Pound Pom' from post-blitz
Birmingham's terraces in black-and-white,
queues for suet and prunes, slag heaps,
pig iron, smelted ore, smokestacks

to the full colour of South Australia's
blue gums, vanilla lilies, rainbow lorikeets,
where you found a husband and your husband
left you with two kids on a nurse's wage

near the wharves of Port Adelaide
where you couldn't have known your road
would loop and weave for six decades further,
hard-worn and beyond with strange troves,

until now. Margaret, if it is true
we exist most in the minds of others,
then you're still on the road from Solihull
to Taperoo. Through Semaphore

where the sea is dolphin-splash blue,
where pelicans guzzle perch whole
and the sky is passionfruit at sundown,
you'll resume knitting among memories

in photos while silver gulls, terns, ibis
birds circle and glide with silent wings
into the far-off, over everywhen waves
that roll across the Gulf of St Vincent.

Asylum

It's one thing to leave your own home
for the hills, under undead stars
without one glance at those left behind,

it's another thing to kick everyone else
out on their arse, out to the winds
and lock your house doors with a big iron bar.

Snow spawns from a dark height,
swarms against the window while you prink
and prim yourself in your empty room,

snowflakes like a swarm of faces
as you're drawn to the curtain-chink
to see your own image amid the spume

in the window: to see your own
outline in the pane, in the gloom,
blurred with teeming legions—

caged in your bright room,
in your hollowed self-reflection,
bemixed by the dark in which you drown.

The Gripes

Your head hits the pillow
and through the duped night
your mind becomes a yoyo
yanked by string so taut

it could slice an apple.
Just as when a body—
whether somebody or nobody—
bites the dust and all

these worms, gnats and maggots,
filthy clouds of flies,
emerge to feast on the meat
within minutes, *wherever* it dies:

so pixels and bytes
fill the air like the spoor
of some grim *Fomori*
until brimming with gripes

that have swarmed out the rectum
of the datasphere,
through your transmission spectrum
so all that you hear, all that's here

is fed on a feedback loop
of ill will that flows
from the tips of your toes
to the tippety-top of your pillow.

The Troll

Maybe somebody, somewhere will see you
for what you are—
a miracle of moods, words
and molecules. In time

you might stick a post-it message
on a fridge door
saying *lasagne inside, love x*
causing someone whose day sucked

to vibe in-sync with your complex
waves and particles.
But, right now, even the birds in the trees
seem to whisper *get fucked*

so why, you ask, should you fight
the itch to track her
updates, typing somebody, somewhere
is watching you, bitch?

By the Burren River

The station phone rings: a weedy voice wants
to confess. *'We were just out, like, for a jaunt*
and he was hitching, dandering on the scrag,
so we picked him up: knew him for a Taig.

'It was a claw hammer. We said we had blow
to get off-road, and we parked in the shadow
of a big bent tree behind a tall scraggly hedge.
I did him in the back of his head.'

Then petrol, blue flames, burnt flesh in the fenlands
of the Mournes and the slip of his body
into a ten-foot water pit where he slept
with crows, sheep, cows, horses, one of thousands.

First Epistle to David

for David Wheatley

My friend, once again we find ourselves
in mean times. Who'd have guessed the twelve
angels of the apocalypse would appear as mere trolls,
dour bots, stark raving online leprechauns
driving sound sense to its grave
and jiggety-jig-jigging on its tombstone?

Remember *The Third Policeman*'s
theory of atomic fusion between human
and bicycle? Well, I'm near certain
my head and backbone,
through demonic consubstantiation,
are now seventy-five percent smartphone.

I've had this recurring dream since childhood:
I'm some kind of cool zen Jedi dude
rebelling against the evil Empire. In the maze-like load-
bay of a galactic warehouse I make my stand.
Then my nemesis turns into a barcode,
says, 'I am your father,' and chops off my hand.

In Patrick McCabe's book *Pogue Mahone*
time after time the question
is asked: 'Why do birds sing?' And it's close to the bone,
the lack of an answer, while life keeps delivering,
as McCabe drives it home,
a 'cough-softening blue fucking Jaysus of a walloping.'

I'd say stuff this, kick back in my easy chair,
but well I know the red arse of anger
would soon flare. We're neither here nor there,
more fuckwads than monads, monetizable subjects
(*ooh-er!*) conducting complex affairs
in words, in worlds, in a world of hallucinated objects.

In the morning they'd have me wake and yell 'Go!
Al! Go!' at myself in the mirror using slick Al-go-
rhythms. In the evening they'd have me lie low,
flubbed in my small room, mind-fizzed like a bath
bomb in bathwater, dreaming of the jet-flowed
hot-tubbing bubbles of death. Sorry, wealth.

I dreamed of a wild passionate affair with Penélope Cruz.
I had a long toxic affair with supermarket booze.
Now I'm in a desolate affair with this fuzz
of gorse, scragged hills, these mazing paths through wild
grass waiting for the night to ooze
over thornbush and pale distant wheatfields.

The sun was always furious
but so far and same-same, we forgot to notice.
The  who lead us
are so nuts for the rush of their profit run
that while existence is snuffed out by the solar furnace
they punch the air shouting: 'We've won! We've won!'

So when your poem came through the post,
my friend, I was lost
once again in a dark swarming forest
of gripes. But reading your verse letter
lifted me, the way a pancake toasts,
raises and forms itself from a gloop of pancake batter.

Yes, as you say, we have reached our autumn.
Now we're here it may well be our function
not to boo-hoo, but keep on, called upon
in view of the abysmal, to find the fol-
de-rol in things. Who knew? Our task to name
what's of worth and reasons to be cheerful.

Good is a road, for example, through a dark green glade
of conifers, their long-haired hypnotised heads
swishing to-and-fro, as if to the Grateful Dead.
Good is the raindrops' music on my window.
Good are the darting navigational doodads
and swoops of the sparrow, or swift, or swallow.

Great are the microbes that might yet generate
mass renewable energy from biomass substrates.
Great is a double duvet with warm dreamers within it.
Great the original horizon
when you're looking out to sea at Ballyhalbert;
and also, the spicy squid from Hot Kungfu takeaway in Newington.

Glorious are purple asters, microchips, a blackbird's chatter.
Glorious the Extinction Rebellion, Black Lives Matter
and #MeToo movements (thank me later, thank me later).
Glorious are froghoppers, slow-swayed hay fields, and lips.
Glorious are sundews, the molecular structure
of DNA, dictionaries, artificial hips,

'Zungo' by Nina Simone, fresh cotton undercrackers,
freckles, Lough Neagh, Lough Tay, face-exploding laughter,
the woman in the rain collecting for Action Cancer
outside the Aldi while sunrays split the dark trouble
of a cloud so it's like you're stood among the thousand and one shimmered
statues of the Goddess of Mercy in Sanjūsangendō Temple.

Precious are cathedrals, schools, hospitals, and those who make
them; precious the peaceful city; and the walk
of toddlers as they teeter and wobbulate and tooter but stalk
on somehow with the big beam of a sunflower
stretching arms out wide—for it is now o'clock
in the heartbeat of our sons, our daughters.

But bad Habbies and tiring threads
can list on. So, as Sam Beckett once said,
ta-ta for now David. I'll look forward to *Child Ballad.*
Cheers for the letter. Cheers for 'Tunnels Through the Head'.
Something stays, keeps shape, in the best of our lines
though everything changes, and that's time.

November 2023

North Street

Sometimes this place gets up my schnozzle—
its smut, smooshed litter, stale fry smoor,
ditched Buckfast bottles weeping at the nozzle.

Then whiffs of bran, Guinness, the pure
perfume of new hair-dos, nut-jobs, do-yer-head-in
kids tugging their Ma's shopping bags, hum their overture.

When the street smears my eyes, flinty and grim,
deeper rhythms of hither and yon assuage:
the shops' wafts of song, snitches of what's spoken—

So that's sausage 'n beans, wi no beans, 'n extra sausage?
I close the windows of my eyes, open
the doors of my ears, let the music in.

Accelerator

Four billion quid for little more
than chucking particles from one element
at the particles of another
with whatever force can be mustered.

Every day is a supercollider—
who knows what's coming round the bend:

me, Stevo and Terry McCoy,
stones like apple cores
in our palms, windowpane cracked,
shaking in our bones by the big house hedge

while the peeler who'd come out of the blue
faster than a bullet up the elm-arched lane
slowly rolls up his sleeve and says, 'Boys,
this is going to hurt me more ...'

By Strangford Lough

in memory of Stephen Vaux Wright

Downcast in North Down on the cusp
of the nineties, Ulster saying nothing
new on each wall, I slumped with a Bass
in the dead Ivy Bar. Then in you burst
as if just moored from dark moon-
bonkered seas on a lough-bobbing boat:
'YES!', you loomed, 'this is AMAZING!'

In Falls' Bar we witnessed someone murder
'Here Comes the Night' on Cookie's Karaoke
sinking pints of Purple Nasty and Snakebite,
you already in that green canvas jacket—
your uniform for the next thirty years—
pumped-up on Lenin or Solzhenitsyn:
we waited for the revolution to begin

in Newtownards. Stevo, you've left too soon.
Look, here's Cheryl and your sons in town.
Soon Bobby and Sam will be young men
down from the Craigantlet hills to find
what the night offers. They'll hold your good
nature the way the waters of the lough
are cradled in the arms of the land.

Feet on the ground, head in the moon:
your big beam in the classroom brightened
the kids you taught. Your grave struggles
to hold down your sunlight
as memories of you lift like a guzzle
of crisp-gleaming pop-cold amber-fizzing apple
cider on a close day. Now here comes the night

over Craigantlet, Cairn Wood, Greengraves.
Doors are locked, a light is put out by someone
pulling curtains. There are shouts and chant-songs,
a stagger of hallions on the town, while a small boat
sets out for the North Channel and darkness
falls across Court Street, The Old Cross, The Ivy,
the moon-lanterned waters of Strangford Lough.

The Aunties

Cured haddock infested the kitchen
where I'd sit at the edge of my Aunts
with their thistle hair, wheaten bread
and breath of Benson and Hedges

listening to atrocities on a short-
wave radio. Stroke, bomb, gun,
cancer—all were the same to them
with their litanies of the dead,

dying, and those struggling to care
for all still needing to be cared for.
Sure ye'll sour the milk with that face!
one Aunt teased me, and the rest yakked

and cackled as the sun crashed through,
cutlery sparkled and the room flashed daft
daffodil, butter-gold, egg-yoke brilliant.
Then one-by-one my Aunties left.

Ards

With nowhere to go I get in the car
and veer downhill in a lowered-window
breeze, May blossom in the air
like a cure for the gripes or whatever

drives me through conifer-lined
roads to the glimmer of the lough
where I park to wonder where on earth.
Diesel after-fumes mingle

with nettle musk and furze-bloom
vanilla while the dusk-stained tide
gleans it has nowhere left to turn

but back. Elms shiver.
Soon all will come to rest
in Greyabbey, Clandeboye, Movilla.

Until the Cows Come Home

I was to man a gap in the boundary
hedge at the curve of the field
to keep cows from breaking through
when they were driven to their dark byre.

A green ten-year-old town-boy
dazed amid a white skimmering
of mayflowers, I thought five or so cows
would dawdle past chewing the cud.

I remember the twitch of that quiet
anticipation—no cars, an odd shout
from cousins in a barn across the mire,
soldier flies tormenting the hedge.

Then they came: a riot of meat
stampeding round the bend in a frenzy
of udders, eye-whites, black tongues—my Uncle
yelling Hold! as I vanished through the gap.

Now field, farm, everyone has passed away
it comes. I wake to cow-reek, gentle snorts
by my bedside, as I rise and follow
through the night sky's burns, glens, bale-fires.

Nuggets

A box of biscuits by the bedside,
pills in a dimpled plastic tray—
your granny lies in her tiny bones
and mumbles, mysterious, while you say nothing,
barely thirteen, blank as the day.

You are keeping an eye on her
breathing, her little bones heaving,
and your eyes scan figurines, mementos,
harrowed fields through the window:
hay barns, small farms, a battery hen shed—

Bwwaaakk! Buck-back-bock-buckaaaakk!—
where rows of chickens queue
under a funnel, hung from a gibbet
swung like a big steel conical conundrum
over their calamity of feathers.

Her weak breath does not reach heaven
but hazes among the chipped figurines,
the TV's blank screen, fading flowers
on the wallpaper, dun as the scrimped wings
of those rows upon rows of throbbing chickens.

Drop one head-first into the funnel
and its head pops through a blood-rimmed *O*
to stare into numbles and giblets
on the floor, onto which it will stream
like warm port, its feet still in a fidget.

What gets passed on, through generations?
Your granny tries to speak, so you bend
your head down. But you'd get more sense
from the sea in a seashell as your Da
enters the room beaming, Well! Well?

Auntie Agnes

I last walked her home
to her small room in November.
Her skin was blemished ice,

the skyline an ice cap
about to calve, ambulance sirens
so frequent they melted

into air. Light as a feather,
the pallbearers remarked.
Tall cranes loomed across the city.

All that we have. Wee calf.
All that is fair, all that
was solid moves through the air.

A Silver Sixpence in Her Shoe

Scuttle at the coal bunker—
            first the shush of coke dust,
then the clump and rolled
            tumble of good big lumps,
jet as rats, raising smut
            clouds and tarry perfume
to mingle with breath-mist
            in the cold bite of the morning,
scraping and scratting
            in the coffin-narrow yard
next to the thin kitchen's
            kettle whistle and steam.

Agnes hopscotches in the back
            alley singing 'My Grand
Ma and Your Grand Ma'
            until her Ma calls, 'Come in
til yer tea,' and in she soodles
            with a screak of the back gate
into the clittering yard,
            dawn smog in her eyes,
into the dank steaming
            kitchen, her aggrieved Ma
at the cold shelf saying,
            'That baste's been at the butter again!'

Five in the bed and one brother
whimpers, 'Gráinne, oh Gráinne!'
Agnes bites back her sniggers,
her head in the armpit
of her sister, who raises
a finger to moonlit lips,
the curtain chinked open
onto factory towers like grim
class teachers looming
over the blackboard of the night:
'Shhh, don't wake us, Agnes,
Da has drink in 'im!'

Ma says, 'We'll get her
married, so help me God.'
'Sure there's bucks droolin' fer her,'
says Auntie Grace. 'Isn't that half
the trouble?' Ma says,
'she's longer legs than sense.'
Agnes lurks on the stairs
twisting a ragdoll's pigtails,
picturing the inner workings
of her sister's mind as tall
scissor-like legs striding
the world in racy stockings.

With three brothers working
        on the docks Agnes
wriggles under the kitchen
        table while her Ma whacks
the fury from mutton bones.
        Outside a chimney spews
fumes like a ship's funnel—
        Belfast a huge ship chugging
through the blue—and when
        Agnes asks, 'Will I sail the high
seas too?' Ma stops skinning
        spuds to sigh, 'Aye, love. Aye.'

'It'll soon jiss be Agnes,'
        says Auntie Grace.
'Mm,' says Ma, over the mangle,
        cardigan smeared with slag
black as Da's socks. Then silence,
        broken as the dock horn
blows time and a river
        of men rush for beer or bibles,
soot clouds lifting
        into the sky. Ma stares
at the wall. 'Soon enough,'
        she mumps, 'they all fly.'

Confetti and embers: Agnes
            kneels by the gleed and crackle
of the fire on this, her sister's
            wedding night, and minds
her dress, her whisper—'Agnes,
            Agnes you could go anywhere.'
She's drifting away from her Da's
            fluty snores, parlour walls
bituminous as porter,
            blending with the night's
stars like frost-flickers
            on coal, sugar on liquorice.

Agnes dream-floats over the clunt
            and rhythm of the city,
glimmerous as the moon
            peering back into her
weeny mid-terrace,
            the lunt of her parlour
at a snoring drunk,
            a small girl kneeling by the host
of the flame, and her Ma
            staring out the window
at the coal-black street
            red-eyed and fleered as a ghost.

The Kamo River in Kyoto

Along the Kamogawa
between Sanjō Bridge and Shijo Bridge
a heron

stands in the stream's
million pieces of mirror-
glinting movement:

a stock-still heron.
Under the motionless sun
that could bake an egg,

listening to the plash
of river-trickle,
standing in the surface-shimmer

like an inscrutable
data centre
surrounded by a million solar panels,

the heron is still.
I remember
Herzog's words, 'I discover

no kinship, no understanding, no mercy.
I can see only
the overwhelming indifference

of nature.' Yet it stands:
a heron
among reed-waver,

potpourri shadows
under Yoshino cherry trees.
A light breeze flutters.

Traffic on Kawabata,
signal noise from Kiyamachi.
The world is changing.

In the on-flow
and flux of eddy swirls
standing motionless:

a heron
between Shijo Bridge and Sanjō Bridge
along the Kamogawa.

The Middle of the Road

in memory of Ken Millard

The football hit a beachball and skewed
into goal, as if to prove how a thing can shift
mid-flight from one point to another point
unforeseeably—and now we're through

with the game, you and your Dad content
in the back as we edge through Roker,
South Shields, avoiding heavy traffic
by the North Sea, with its ominous intent,

pointing to landmarks from your life here
long ago—before joining this road North
that bores across fields, narrow rivers, thin
country lanes, where we shift through the gears

yet feel as if we're ants crawling up the mid-
rib of a sprawling leaf's network of veins;
and when I whinge about the length of the road
you claim all the pleasure's in being mid-

way: how you relish a trek through the so-so,
a long trip through nowhere in particular—
say, from Phoenix, or El Paso—where the point's
to linger anywhere, and pass through slow.

All I know is that it's been a fine day
despite the score. Thousands upon thousands
rising from thin terraced streets towards
the turnstiles, turning at the end of play

from the sadness of an emptying stadium
to vanish into Sunderland, the hinterlands
of Tyne and Wear, Northumberland; and now
we're driving through the Borders, the tedium

offset by your tales of Texan Motels and corn
fields bigger than Glasgow, the strange glow of all-
night Diners, as we drive under dusk-deep plum
skies of falling leaves, past shaken blackthorn,

wind-bent ash trees, leaf-swirls and bungalows,
farmhouses, road signs pointing to improbable
place names where small birds zigzag and swoop
among the scattering leaves—swifts or swallows

turning by twilight into shadows.
Soon enough, we'll say goodbye to your father,
thank each other for the day it has been.
And for years after, Ken, I will follow

your lead: to savour the style in the non-
descript and abide in the particular mundane.
But now we are streaming through a darkhead
of sorrow, harvested fields, here and gone

and passing all too fast, for it is late
and this road we're on stretches
from Edinburgh's Crags, the shores of the Forth
to South Shields, Roker, the Stadium of Light.

Virus

The airports are silent—no Emirates, no Delta,
no skies stained by EasyJet, Jet2, Lufthansa.

The train departing King's Cross station is empty;
no passengers spewed from the Cairnryan ferry.

No one enters Coldstream, or leaves Invergordon.
Roads are clear through Perth, Fife, Midlothian.

Not a peep in Muirhouse, or Drylaw, or Pilton.
You'd hear a pin drop in Prestonfield and Moredun.

Along Ravenswood Avenue and Redgauntlet
Terrace—Hazeldean, Glenallen, Glenvarloch

Crescent—nothing approaches. Pull the blinds.
No. 35. No soul stirs. 37. Night looms. 39.

Waiting Rooms

The Covid dead are waiting to be processed.
Having collected a ticket on arrival
they sit and wait for their number to be called:
rows upon rows of them, out of politeness
trying not to show they are peeved.

The Covid dead are lonely, but in most cases
friendly. 'Hard to believe,' Harry says to a new
neighbour, 'we were planning an anniversary
trip to Keswick. Five days later, I'm here!'
There are no windows, but it's a nice touch,

the calming azaleas, even if synthetic.
Some of the Covid dead have formed
local groups, making plans to haunt relatives
with guidance on vaccines, for next time.
Jade misses her husband's chicken supreme.

There are no clocks, and they've been waiting
so long, time is doing funny things.
Cynthia, who'd always been a bit spiky,
to be fair, now finds herself drawn to listen
to others. She softly pats Colin's hand.

Brian misses the lads, and will support
Rangers forever, but he's entranced
by distant chatter from the international zones
soothing over him like a fabulous river.
He tries to remember Dawn's face.

Wings and blocks, row upon row
of waiting rooms stretch further
than the eye can see, zone after zone,
for the numbers of the Covid dead
exceed the population of Rio.

Few of the Covid dead are in pain now,
although Chuck from Florida's stomach
still burns after injecting Clorox Clean-up.
When someone's number is called they pass through
a door. No one can see the other side

but for a moment you can glimpse bright cloud.
Deborah imagines the waiting rooms
and all in them are floating through the void
like a space station spinning around and around.
When someone is called the rest smile

and sit, wondering how their loved ones
are keeping, or if the daffodils came
up nicely last Spring. Or something
completely different. For the wait goes on
and the Covid dead are not the same.

Killynether Wood

I

Hard to believe I'm here, not just in my head,
in this green, so green I'm dizzy,
lockdown now lifted after so long, so many
added to the numbers of the dead.

Now I can't get my head around these ferns,
hazel, stipple-dappled leaves of beech
and wavy bluebell carpets, more strange
than ever, but never so welcome.

It's like there's been some big cosmic download
and here's this: hazel wood, bluebells, beech,
a linnet's burble—like the soundtrack in your head
when you try to imagine inner peace—

thickets and clearings, nettles, celandine:
now dark olive, now whisky-dram,
now canary-glare. It is May, 2021.
Everything scrolls through the mind

and it's hard to shake off the room-and-screen-
and-click, click-and-screen-and-room
routine, even here, amid this lift-and-dip motion
as if the mind is breathing, and woods dream.

2

Hard to believe that photo still fades
on my parents' wall, still in its slant frame—
1981 that might have been—
smiling blank amid fernbrake and leafglade

with my two sisters
in our nylon elastic Sunday best
perched on a dead tree trunk to pose
for a 'just act natural' family picture.

Once hung on the wall, aged eight, I could see
we were aliens out of place, out of time—extras
in a regional drama—
and I've since mused on my 'separate phantasy'

until this moment. As if in a trance.
Hard to believe this, now, is the same place
where my big sister in a dress of powder blue
smiled below beech trees that swayed as if to woo

the breeze, and my wee sister in a pinafore
of lemon turned away with a sulk
while, from some blast or other, Belfast smoke
rose behind the photographer.

3

No one else around. From this beech and hazel
I feel *something*, as if the air itself bears
a trace of all that has been dreamed here,
an archive beyond the tangible

like whatever was in that microdot
on the tip of Josie McBurney's tongue
when we lay in a nook, away from the throng
of White Lightning drinkers out of their pots

on poppers and speed that smelled of Ariel
Automatic while gunfire from Belfast
sounded over the hills, mingling with blasts
from ghetto-blasters of The Orb, or Orbital,

me and Josie zoning in on a complex
mingling of spleenwort and meadow-rue,
peach skies, homeless clouds, common blues,
my insides feeling like forty pounds of Semtex

watching friends over this green horizon
crack their nuts—1991
this might have been—coming down from the hazel
to vanish into bluebells at sundown.

4

Hard to believe, now I'm here, these bluebells
and I can't help thinking about how I should be
feeling. Bumbazed, I tell myself to be
in-sway with the moment, *au fait* with bluebells

but even before that family photo was hung on the wall
and I realised we were in human disguise—
not what we seemed, even to ourselves—
I sensed something was up. Though beautiful,

a day of sunburst green-yellow musical notations,
my sisters bluebell-picking,
I could feel myself apart even while partaking
while smoke from some plastic explosion

rose from Belfast to drift across North Down's
satellite towns, potato drills, fields of barley,
council zones, conifer woods and carriageways
in a flume of particulates and cyclonite toxins

that circled and lingered in these architraves
of beech, seeping into the rhizoplane
to dinge and bane the entire ecosystem
from root-creepers to intricate leaves.

5

On Google Earth it looks like broccoli
florets. But this is a grove cathedral
of beech, fern and hazel,
scintillations under the canopy.

Now I'm here it's hard to believe
this hazel on the ever-sloped side
of Scrabo Hill is the same under which me and Josie slid
back in a nook of sprouting leaves,

sapped roots, vines like tangled hair
on a mattress of twig-fall and feather-moss,
pollinated catkins like mysterious
tongues, tingled leaves filtering the air

into which a linnet
now rises above the beech and hazel
over barley fields, market towns, yellow pimpernel,
redevelopment zones, cattle byres and crisis-hit

care homes with oxygen concentrators and corridors
of chlorine where my sister donned her Personal Protection Equipment
and day-by-day tried to put a halt
to the vulnerable, in strange beds, becoming numbers.

6

While dead numbers rose I was in the clutch
of a room-and-screen-and-click, click-and-screen-
and-room routine, self-pitying, demeaned
because unable to interpret, or make felt, or deeply feel much,

dreaming my room darkened to vine-tips,
fern tongues, musky darkgreen nettles
in a hutch of broom, mast and sprintles.
Now split me open, and a storm of thrips

will swarm and scar the earth,
yet these purled pools of blue-
bells do indeed wave like 'the blue
sky breaking up through the earth'.

Here we were, my sisters, and here they are—
the wildflowers we waded through once before
in pools of violet flowing nowhere
as the photographer clicked to capture

these multi-trillion particles mingling together
with us in their midst, the way things that are
fold within themselves things that were,
and might be. Here in Killynether.

In the Garden

Everywhere I go there's a circumference
somewhere. July is here.

A bee is up to its backside in the cornflower.
Trees become tree-shadows in the dusk.

Each day I've less of a clue.
A blue-speckled butterfly flutters and flaps

hither and thither and I think to myself:
'Yup.' An end is nigh.

Or tomorrow.
Seagulls circle like wrong-coloured crows

and the sun is inconceivable
in its particular detail,

yet falls. The smell of mown grass,
children grow older.

A cat flits through a hedgerow.
Gently, into darkness, into what-will-it-be.

Walking Out One Morning

Darkness everywhere. Night pervades, then dies.
Now kerb sweepers, bread vans and early traffic
rumble by my window-side bed while rain-music
fizzles on slate roofs as dawn pours inside.
An alarm squawks that I must not lie
in my listening to telegraph-pole birds getting high
over elms and rowans, lifting into citrus-burst skies
like memories of songs, but rise
and walk the city with multimillioned windows for eyes.

Versions of the world and time are limned
through screens over-pinging with messages.
Data flutters through whatever dimension it is
data flutters through—the space within
space, as I open my door like a book
and walk past steam-wands stretching hot-foamed milk
in cafés, unshuttering shops, skinnymalink
cats curled under fenceposts, the lampposts' travelogues
of scent casting spells over all-sniffing dogs.

Nothing feels real if it's not on the net
yet nothing on the net feels real.
Now I brim with yesteryears, feeling virtual
on this thoroughfare, walking into carbon debt
and exhaust brume on compact streets dwarfed on each side
by tall grey buildings so the traffic's like a two-lane-wide
ant trail up the deep crack of a rhino's back hide.
And onto grass I go, over the sluice-sounds of drain flow,
underground culverts, into the city meadows.

'One thing is for sure,' he said. Then he died.
Then another. And another. Such vast
scale, my mind miniature. I dreamt I was asked,
by a smart machine, why it shouldn't pull the plug
on human things, and all my consciousness
could muster was spaghettied emotional mess.
Now ping-ponged between position and sense,
onto grass I go: as if the best way of honouring
the dead is to make the most of living.

A teen gobs a humongous bruise-yellow yinger
onto a tree-lined path, and onto grass I go
to sync with the time zone of earth's slow
verbs, dreaming names, faint signals, green whispers,
winged singers in sycamores, willows, hornbeams,
free park benches where a red-headed businesswoman
in an ink-blue suit eats a meal-deal Wiltshire ham
sandwich under clearing heavens while sad shadows
blend with the cherry trees' ginger-tinged sunglow.

Onto grass I go, and I've made it to the meadows.
You'll know, of course, I write this at my desk
in the night, these words already processed
by machine, as a cyclist in look-at-me lycra torpedoes
past a duffel-coated toddler who's learning new words,
links with the living and dead, holding in titchy hands
a dandelion whose wind-drifted seeds land
their trance-like parachutes on bittercress and wild carrot
while a frisbee glides past like a complex experiment

on motion and grace. Through the tree-leaf-reeled
air come soft-pocked tennis sounds, and I can't grasp
this slide between phantom and real, but want to ask,
Hey there, smart machine, how do you feel?
Hey trees, what are you laughing at?
Two students in beanie hats with tote bags of books
sip from reusable refilled hot polypropylene cups,
sunlight on their faces, and yes, I'm in this, whatever it is,
this blue lift, this light page, this world-plunge, this ...

Acknowledgements and Notes

Grateful acknowledgement is made to the following publications in which some of these poems, or versions of them, were published first: *Poetry*, *Poetry Ireland Review*, *Poetry London*, *Subtropics*, and the *Times Literary Supplement*.

Love and gratitude to Wendy, Vincent, and Rosie. Heartfelt thanks to Peter Fallon and all at The Gallery Press, and to Alex Muller and Jeff Holdridge at Wake Forest University Press.

'Midsummer'–with a nod to the ending of 'Pipistrelle' by Mark Doty ('A word in your ear, says the night').

'The Queensferry Bridge'–'Clearly I know, the mind is mountains, rivers, and the great earth; sun, moon, and stars' (Dōgen).

'When You Are Old'–after Yeats, after Ronsard.

'The Troll'–'Even the birds in the trees seemed to whisper ...' from 'Jason the Unpopular' by Lubricated Goat (*Plays the Devil's Music*, 1987).

'By the Burren River'–in memory of James Morgan who was murdered, aged sixteen, in similar circumstances in July 1997.

'First Epistle to David'–'Tunnels Through the Head' is a poem from David Wheatley's book *The President of Planet Earth* (2017). His book *Child Ballad* was published in December 2023 by Carcanet and in May 2024 by Wake Forest University Press.

'The Kamo River in Kyoto'–the Werner Herzog quotation is from his documentary film *Grizzly Man* (2005).

'The Middle of the Road' – on Saturday 17 October 2009, Darren Bent scored a goal for Sunderland against Liverpool, at the Stadium of Light: his shot deflected off a beachball that had been thrown onto the pitch. Sunderland won the game 1–0.

'Killynether Wood' – with a few echoes from 'Mount Blanc' by Shelley; 'like the blue sky breaking up through the earth' (Tennyson).